Doctor Strange is a powerful sorcerer.
What cool magic is he thinking of?

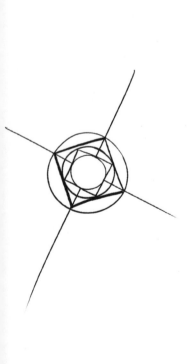

Help Groot hide.
Draw some trees and bushes around him.

Rocket has built a new invention.
What does it look like?

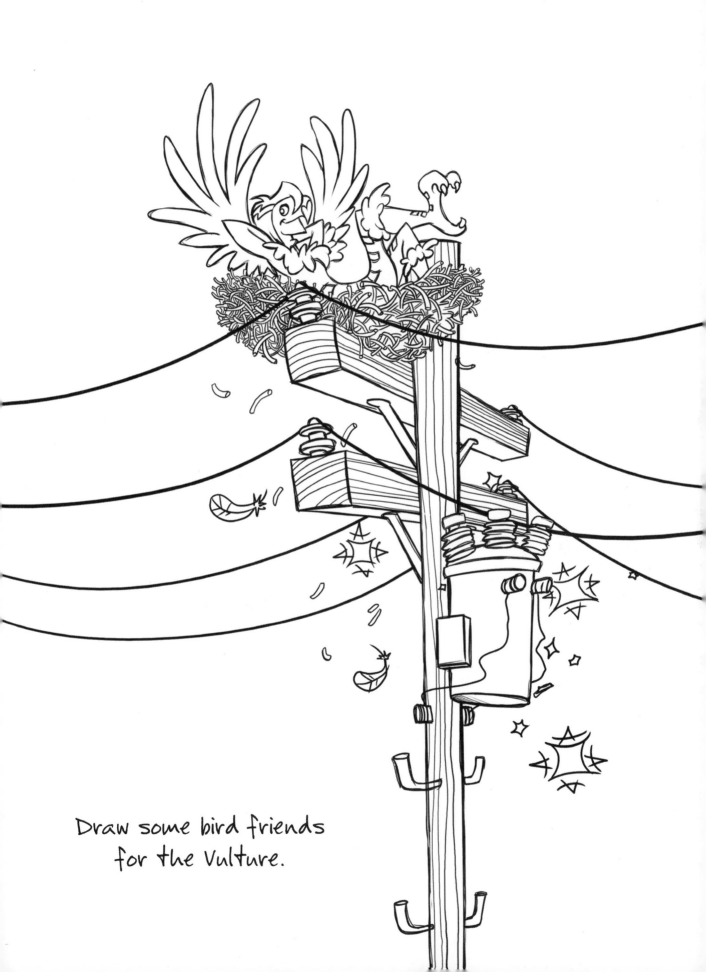

Draw some bird friends
for the Vulture.

Iron Man has made some new boots.
Draw them.

Cap has a new shield.
What does it look like?

Falcon needs some new wings.
Draw them.

Spider-Man wants a new pattern on his costume.
Make it look AWESOME!

Rocket accidentally crashed the Milano,
and the Guardians of the Galaxy have
to use a replacement.

Draw their new ship!

The Chitauri are attacking New York City!
Draw their attack ships.

Draw an awesome new hairstyle
for Black Widow.

Star-Lord got some new headphones.
What do they look like?

Gamora needs
a new sword.
Draw one for her.

Draw Groot growing from this pot.

I am
Grot

What is Hulk smashing?

Draw Black Widow's cool new ride.

Ultron needs a new body.
What should it look like?

Thor has lost his hammer.
Which tool should he use instead?

What is Spider-Man
hanging from?

Loki is up to no good again.
What mischief has he caused this time?

Hawkeye is practising shooting his arrows.
How many arrows have hit the targets?

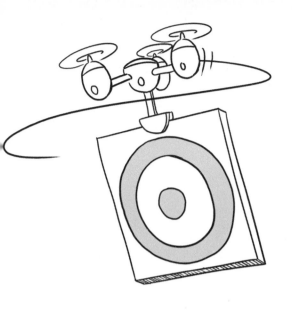

Draw Asgard's beautiful skyline.

Arnim Zola wants to grow a moustache.
Draw him a good one.

The Milano has lost a wing. Draw in a replacement.

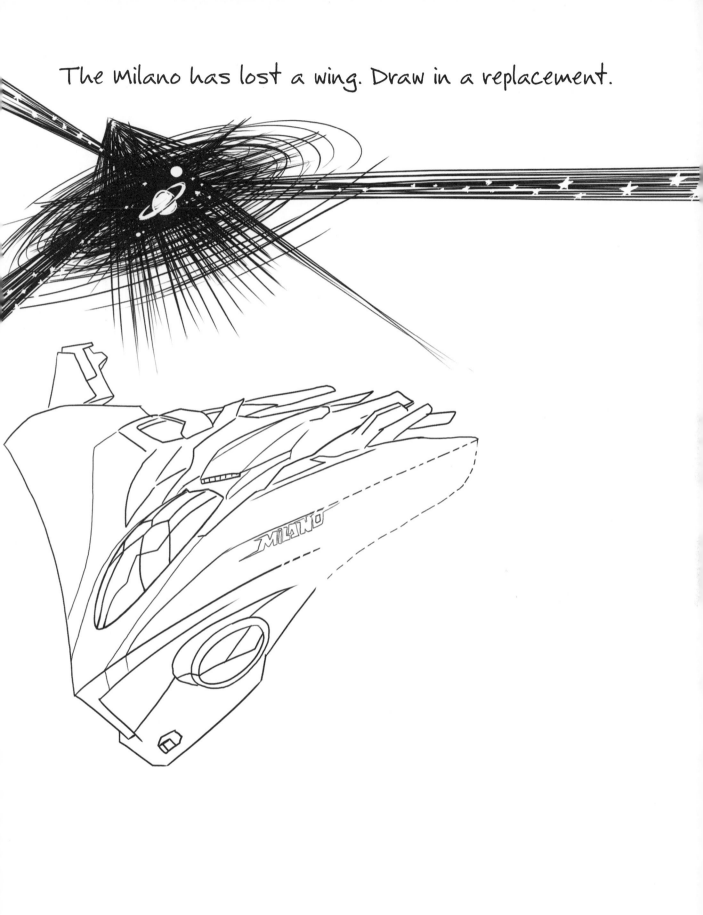

Iron Man has new Hulkbuster armour.
What does it look like?

Doctor Octopus has lost his tentacles.
Draw four new ones for him.

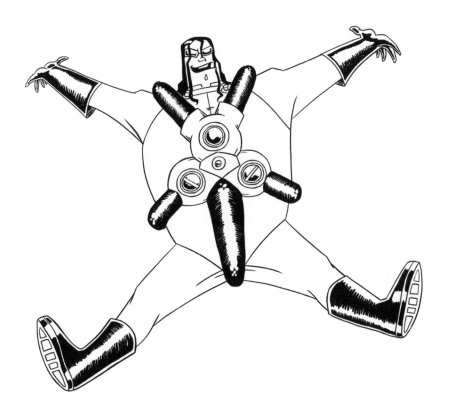

Red Skull has a new device
to use to dominate the world.
What does it look like?

What does the Rainbow Bridge
to Asgard look like?

Thor has a fancy new cape.
Add some cool designs.

Draw Star-Lord's blaster fire ...
and what he is blasting!

What has Spider-Man caught in his web?

It's spring and Groot has started
growing fruit from his limbs.
What kind is it?

What did Hulk break this time?
Oh, Hulk.

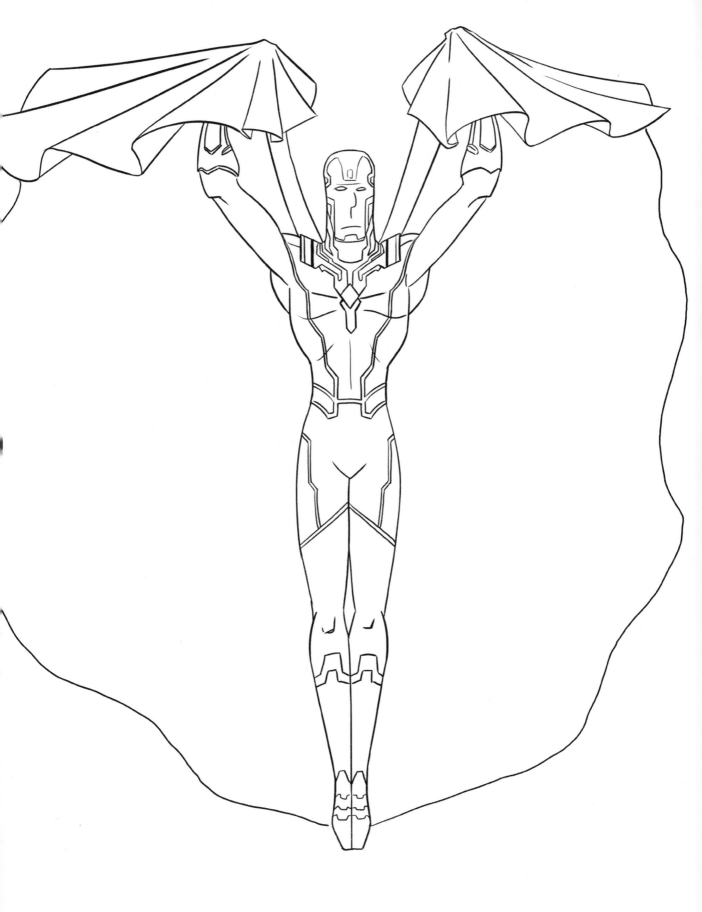

Help Vision decorate his cape.

Draw a helicopter so Spidey can
escape the Sinister Six!

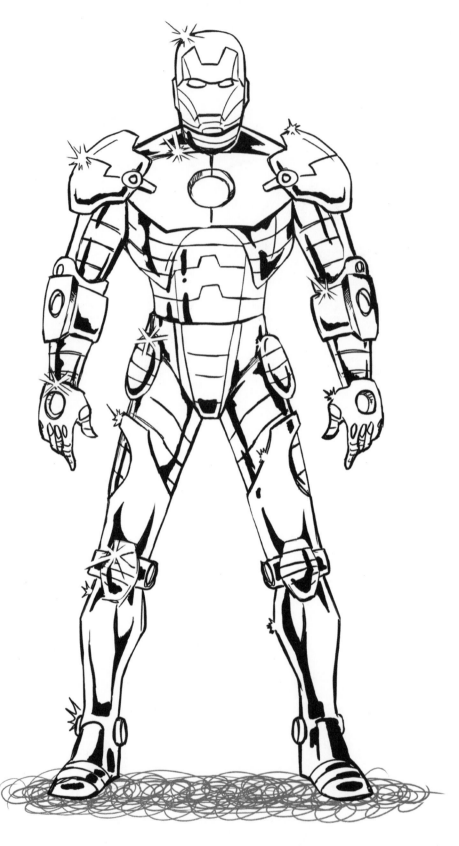

Give Iron Man some really cool
armour modifications.

Steve Rogers needs to get with the times.
Give him a new hairstyle.

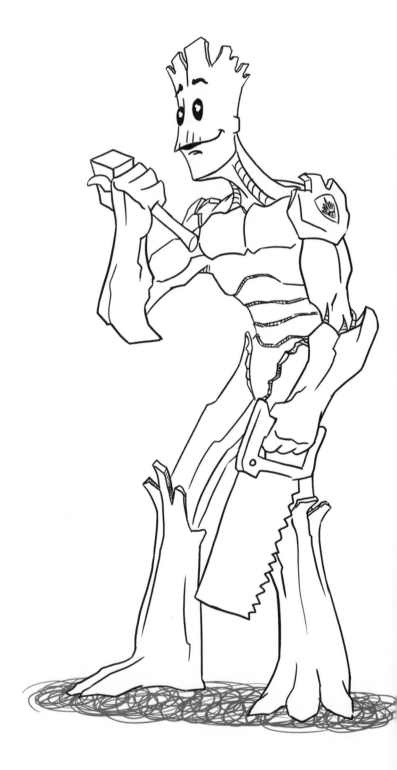

Groot has taken up woodwork.
What did he build?

Drax has no sense of humour.
Go wild with doodles!

What did Gamora just cut in half?
Try not to be too gross.

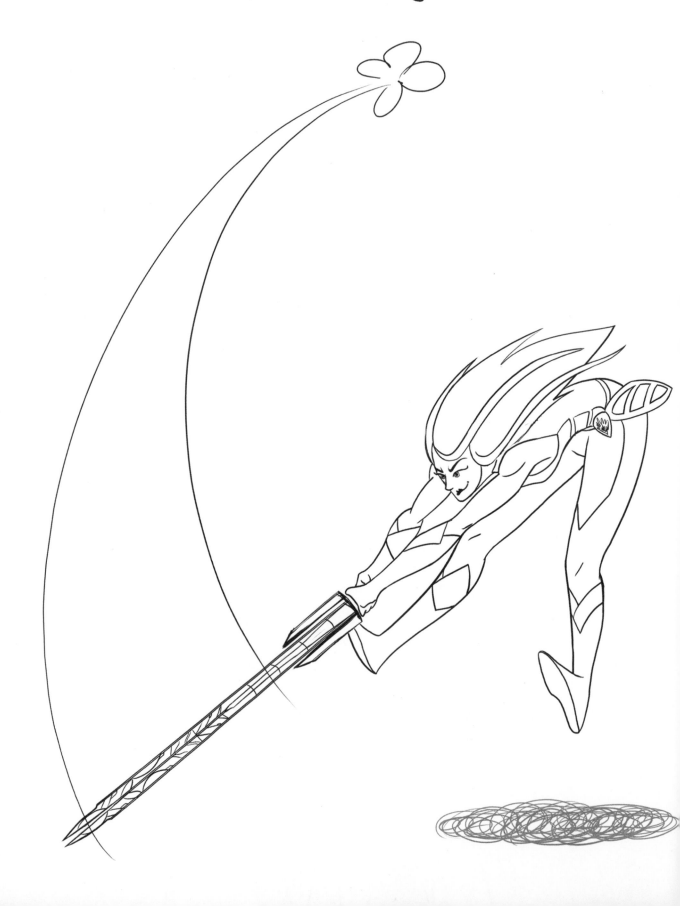

Look how small Ant-Man is! Draw lots
of tiny ants to keep him company.
How many can you draw?

Nick Fury has crashed the
S.H.I.E.L.D. Helicarrier again.
Draw a new one for him.

Help Red Skull build a new evil lair,
but don't make it very good.
He's a bad guy, remember!

Dress up these Chitauri invaders.
Make 'em look snazzy.

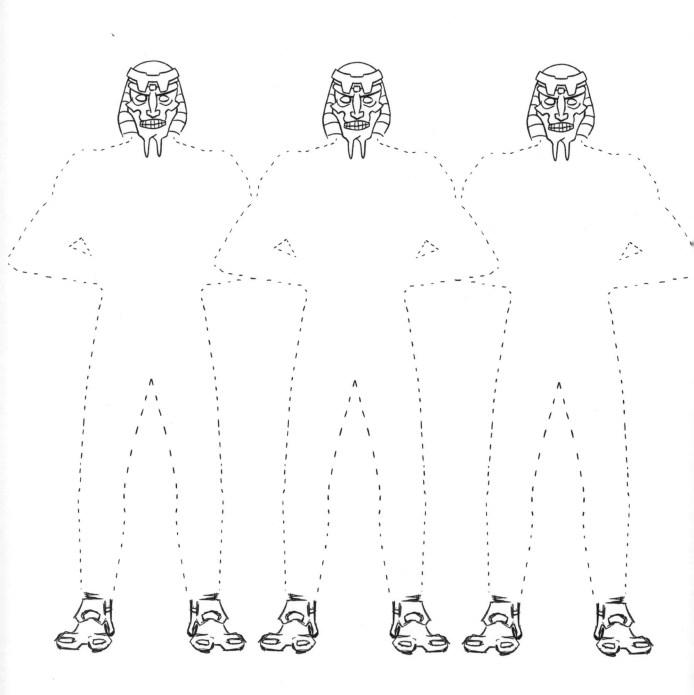

Draw Iron Man's repulsor fire.
Maybe some explosions, too!

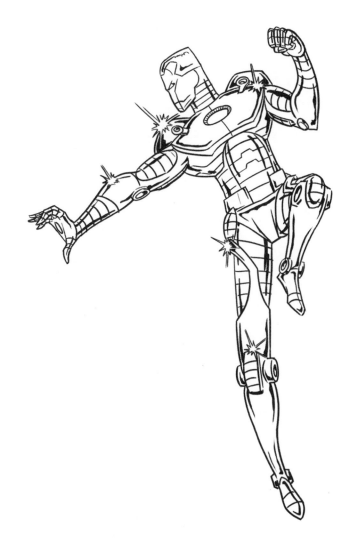

Luke Cage is wearing a new shirt.
Make it funky!

Spidey has lost his mask.
Quick! Draw a new one for him.

Ms Marvel has super-stretchy arms.
Draw them.

Draw stars and explosions to help
the Avengers defeat Ultron.

Draw some magic to help Doctor Strange
defeat Baron Mordo.

Draw some webs to stop Doc Ock!

What is Black Panther jumping over?

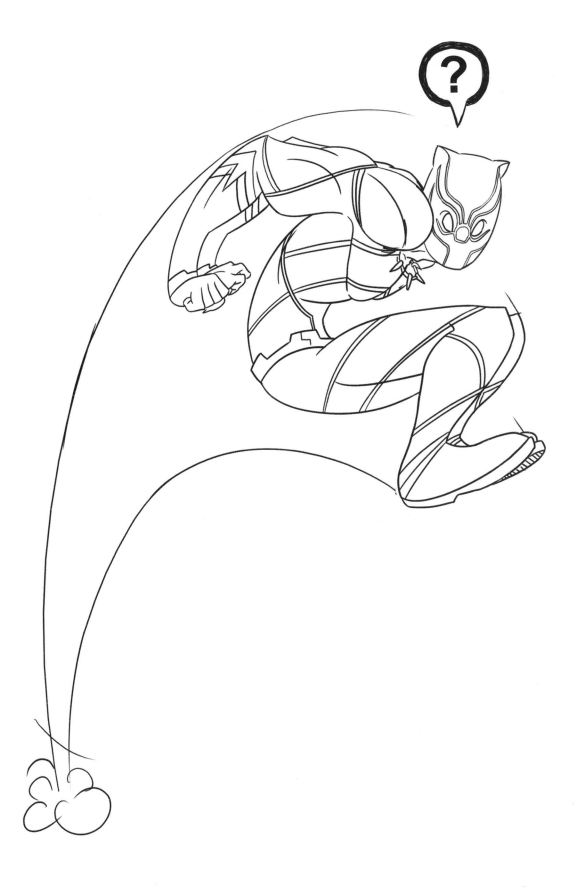

Give the
Winter Soldier
a cool new disguise.

Draw lots of zigzags
to show the lightning
coming from
Thor's hammer.

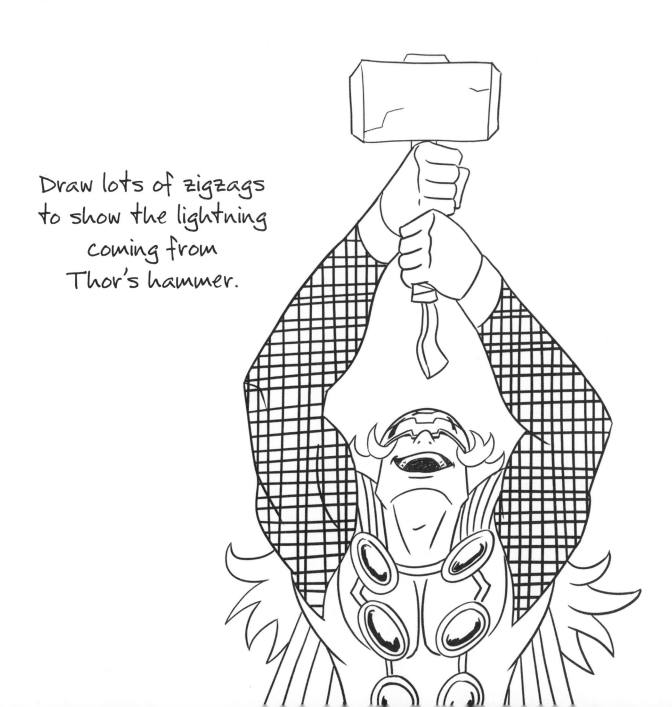

Kraven has caught something in his cage trap.
What did he capture?

Electro is using his electricity
to power a thingamajig.
What is it?

Draw POWS! and stars to help the Guardians of the Galaxy defeat the Chitauri invaders.

You've been working on a new
invention in Tony's R & D lab.
Draw it here.

Ant-Man is flying on a creepy-crawly bug.
What does it look like?

Hint: it has twelve eyes!

Doctor Strange is flying through another dimension.
What does it look like? Who lives there?

Spider-Man, Ant-Man and Black Widow just
came up with a cool Super Hero name.
Draw the new logo here.

Peter Parker took
a picture of Iron Man
battling a villain.
Draw Iron Man's opponent!

The Guardians of the Galaxy are on holiday.
Where did they go?

What's the first thing that pops into
your head when you think of Thor?
Draw it in sixty seconds!

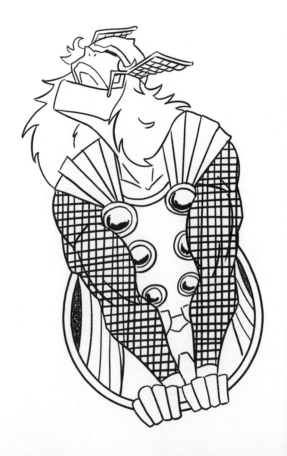

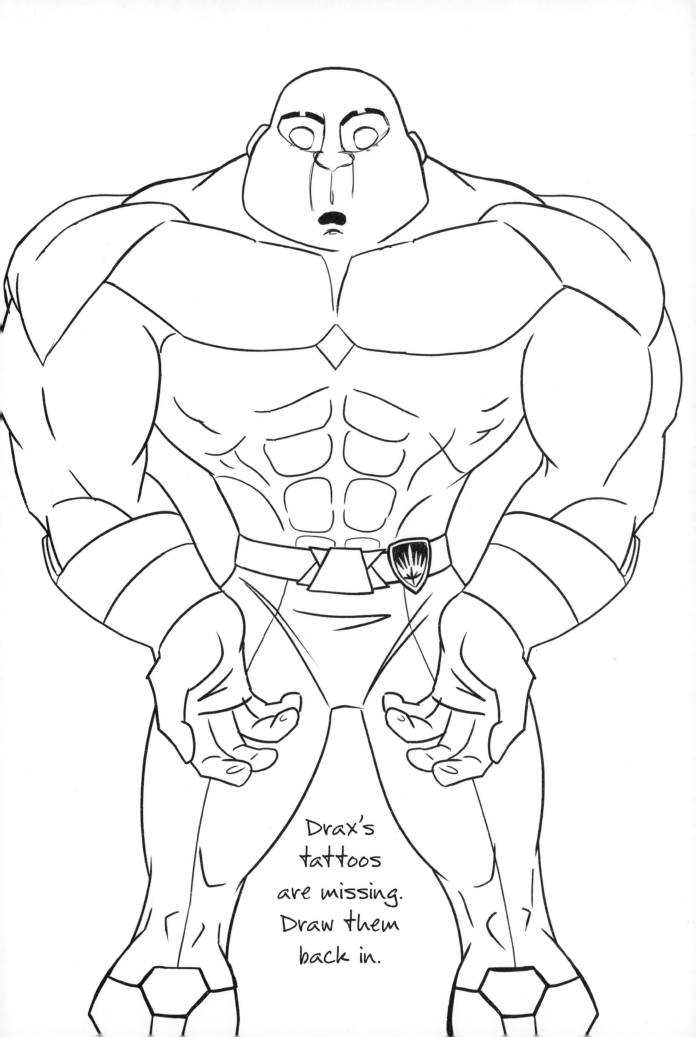

Drax's tattoos are missing. Draw them back in.

The Avengers need a new base.
Draw what it should look like.

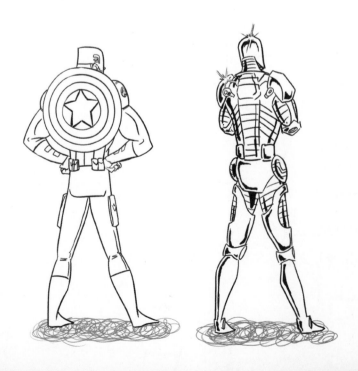

Spidey is after a new villain!
Draw the baddie's face on the poster
to help Spider-Man find him or her.

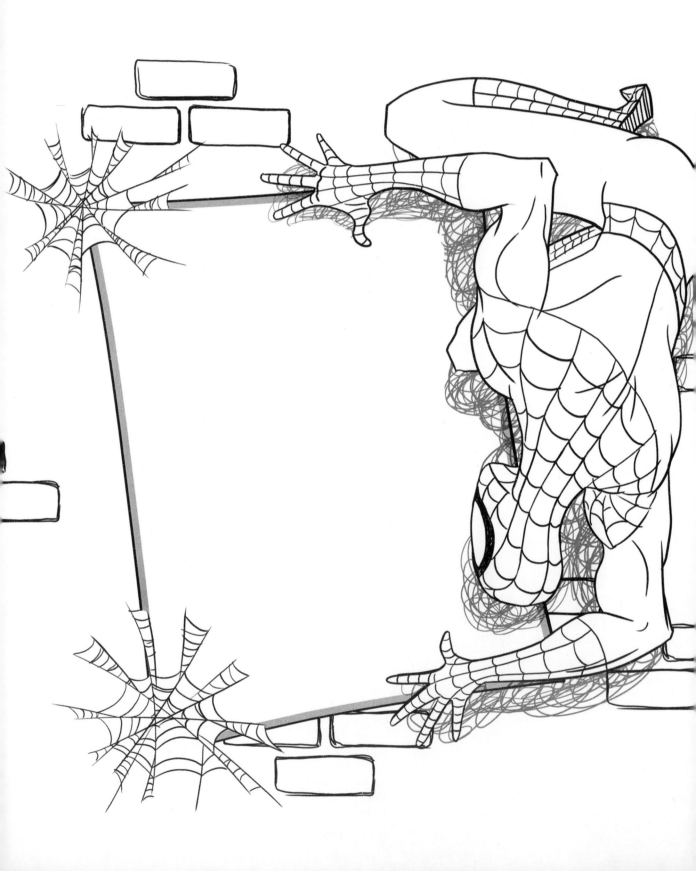

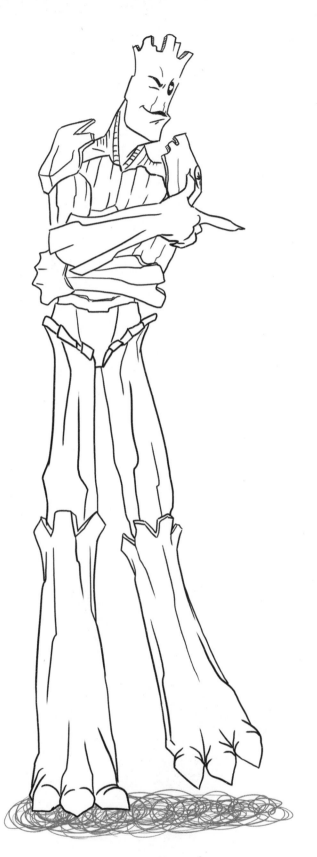

Groot only says "I AM GROOT".
If you could say only one thing, what would it be?
Draw yourself and your favourite phrase.

Doctor Strange loves magic.
Draw a rabbit coming out of the big top hat.

Tony just bought a brand-new boat
for himself and his fellow Avengers.
What does it look like?

Hulk smashed through a villain's hideout.
What's on the other side of the wall?

Spidey used his webs to make a statue.
What does it look like?

Draw the New York skyline.

Star-Lord has new boot thrusters.
What do they look like?

Whoa! Hulk is super strong!
Draw lots of stuff for him to lift.

Draw you and a group
of your favourite Super Heroes!